WEEKLY WR REA
EARLY LEARNING LIBRARY

How People Lived in America

Travel
in American History

by Dana Meachen Rau

Reading consultant:
Susan Nations, M.Ed.,
author/literacy coach/
consultant in literacy development

Please visit our web site at: www.garethstevens.com
For a free color catalog describing Weekly Reader® Early Learning Library's list
of high-quality books, call 1-800-542-2595 (USA) or 1-800-387-3178 (Canada).
Gareth Stevens Publishing's fax: (877) 542-2596

Library of Congress Cataloging-in-Publication Data

Rau, Dana Meachen, 1971-
    Travel in American history / by Dana Meachen Rau.
      p. cm. — (How people lived in America)
    Includes bibliographical references and index.
    ISBN-10: 0-8368-7210-X ISBN-13: 978-0-8368-7210-1 (lib. bdg.)
    ISBN-10: 0-8368-7217-7 ISBN-13: 978-0-8368-7217-0 (softcover)
    1. Transportation—United States—History—Juvenile literature.
  2. Travel—United States—History—Juvenile literature. I. Title.
  HE203.R38 2007
  388.0973—dc22   2006008633

This edition first published in 2007 by
Weekly Reader® Early Learning Library
An Imprint of Gareth Stevens Publishing
1 Reader's Digest Rd.
Pleasantville, NY 10570-7000 USA

Editor: Barbara Kiely Miller
Art direction: Tammy West
Cover design and page layout: Kami Strunsee
Picture research: Sabrina Crewe

Picture credits: Cover, title page, pp. 6, 8, 9, 10, 11, 12, 15, 16, 20 The Granger Collection,
New York; p. 4 © Jeff Greenberg/PhotoEdit; pp. 7, 14 © North Wind Picture Archives; p. 13
© Nancy Carter/North Wind Picture Archives; pp. 17, 18, 19, 21 © Bettmann/CORBIS

Printed in the United States of America

2 3 4 5 6 7 8 9 10 09 08 07

Table of Contents

Cover: Some early cars had side steps to help people get in and out of them.

Travel Today

Today, we can travel across the United States by airplane. The trip takes only a few hours. But people who lived long ago could only dream of flying. Crossing the country took them days, weeks, or even months!

Airplanes have maps that show the states they will fly over on a trip.

Long ago, people . . .

- ❥ did not travel by car;
- ❥ did not travel by bus;
- ❥ did not travel by train;
- ❥ did not fly in airplanes;
- ❥ could travel using only the power of their feet, horses, or the wind.

Children who lived three hundred years ago walked to school.

Travel in Early America

The first English **settlers** came to America in the 1600s. Many people lived in small towns. They could walk to their churches and schools. People who lived on farms could walk to their fields. Most early settlers did not travel very far from home.

Most people used horses to travel longer distances. Families rode on wagons pulled by horses. Horses also pulled carts filled with supplies. Many roads started as trails. As more people used them, the trails became smoother and wider. But when it rained, the roads were muddy. Wagons often became stuck in the mud.

People used early roads to ride to town and church.

PHILADELPHIA IN THE OLDEN TIME.

Ships brought many visitors to the city of Philadelphia.
They sailed up the Delaware River.

People also traveled on rivers and lakes. They rode on
wooden rafts, canoes, or boats. Some people sailed or
paddled from town to town to trade **goods**. Many cities
were built along the **banks,** or edges, of these rivers.

People took **stagecoaches** for long trips. They paid money to ride a stagecoach from one city to another. Some trips took many days. The **passengers** sat inside the stagecoach. A driver sat up front or on top and drove the horses. A stagecoach ride could be a long, bumpy trip!

On long trips, a stagecoach stopped in places where the passengers could eat and rest.

The city of Philadelphia paved many of its roads with bricks. Its sidewalks were made of bricks, too.

In the early 1800s, most roads in America were still made of dirt. People started to **pave**, or cover, some roads with stones or tiny rocks. Traveling was easier on paved roads. Wagon wheels no longer hit big rocks or got stuck in mud.

Bringing America Together

People started to **explore** the land in the West. In 1804, Meriwether Lewis and William Clark began a trip. They traveled west by boat, on horses, and on foot. They drew maps of where they went. Soon, families wanted to settle in the West. They followed each other in wagons and on horses. Long lines of wagons heading west were called **wagon trains**.

People going west in wagon trains traveled during the day. They camped at night.

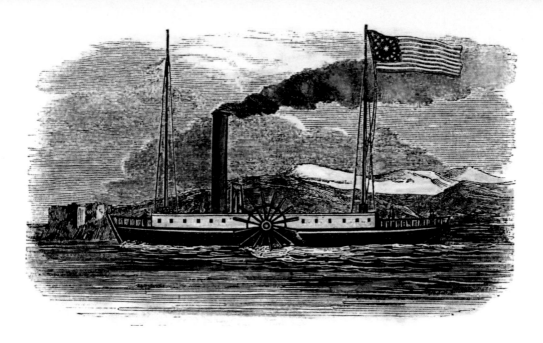

The first successful steamship was named the *Clermont*. It was invented by Robert Fulton.

People started to use **steam** to run machines. The first trip on a **steamboat** was made in 1807. With steamboats, trips that used to take months now took only a few days. People could visit places they had never seen! They could use steamboats to carry supplies from city to city.

Railroads made travel even faster. Railroad companies started to lay train tracks in the late 1820s and the 1830s. **Steam engines** pulled trains through mountains and valleys. They sped through forests and fields. A train trip was ten times faster than traveling by horse and wagon.

A steam engine was strong enough to pull many train cars. The engine left a trail of steam and smoke behind it.

© Nancy Carter/North Wind Picture Archives

The dining cars on some trains were like fancy restaurants.

Early train rides were dangerous. Trains and their tracks, or **rails**, were poorly built and did not use many signals. Trains ran into each other or off the tracks. Stronger rails, better brakes, and signals made trains safer. More people took long trips on trains. They ate fancy meals in dining cars. They slept overnight in train cars with special beds.

In 1869, two train tracks were joined together in Utah. These tracks connected railroads in the East with railroads in the West. Now people could travel all the way across the country by train. Towns grew up along railroad lines. People who lived hundreds of miles away could visit and sell goods.

The joining of the two train tracks in Utah was an important day. People could now travel across the country in just ten days.

State Street is a busy street in Chicago. In 1905, streetcars ran down the middle of the street.

On the Streets

In cities, many people still walked from place to place. But some people rode in **carriages** pulled by horses. Cities grew bigger in the late 1800s. New inventions changed how people could move around a city. People in Richmond, Virginia, were the first to ride an electric **streetcar**. People in Boston could ride an underground train called a **subway**.

The first cars in the United States were built in the 1890s. Early cars were called horseless carriages. They were hard to make and cost a lot of money. Henry Ford invented a new, faster way to make cars. More people could now afford to buy cars. By the late 1920s, many people were driving Ford's Model T cars.

A brand new Model T car rolled through the Ford factory. The car was the fifteen millionth made.

These houses were built in the suburb of Levittown, New York. They looked a lot alike.

People who owned cars could live farther from their jobs. Cities were getting crowded, and some people wanted more space. In the 1950s, people started moving to **suburbs**. A suburb is a town built near a large city. The people without cars could ride streetcars from the suburbs to the cities.

In the 1950s, many **highways** were built to connect cities. People could travel on highways at fast speeds without stopping. Buses already traveled from state to state. Now, buses used highways to take people on longer trips. Some people drove cars on trips across America. Trucks used highways to carry goods across the country.

Gas stations were built along highways. People on long trips could buy gas quickly and then be on their way.

Wilbur Wright watched his brother Orville make the first flight in their airplane. Wilbur flew the plane that day, too

In the Air

The sky became a travel route, too. In 1903, Wilbur and Orville Wright made the first airplane that flew. The brothers' plane stayed in the air for only twelve seconds. Soon, other people built bigger airplanes. These planes could stay in the air longer.

Soon, people could buy tickets to travel on an airplane. Jet airplanes were built in the 1950s. Each plane could carry almost two hundred people. A trip that used to take months now took only a few hours. People living in America could now travel faster and farther than ever before.

The first airplanes were small, but few people flew in them.

Glossary

carriages — wagons pulled by horses with seats for the driver and passengers

explore — to travel to a new place to discover what is there

goods — things, such as tools or food, that you can buy or trade for

highways — paved roads without stops made for cars and trucks to travel fast

passengers — people riding in a vehicle, such as a wagon, car, or airplane

settlers — people who move to and develop a new area

stagecoaches — large covered carriages that are pulled by horses

steam — power from hot water vapor, or gas, under pressure

steam engines — engines that are powered by steam. A train's steam engine is at the front of a train and pulls the other train cars.

steamboat — a boat that is powered by a steam engine

streetcar — an electric train that runs on tracks and carries people on city streets at set times

subway — a train that runs on tracks under the ground.

For More Information

Books

Conestoga Wagons. Richard Ammon (Holiday House)

Stagecoach: The Ride of a Century. Building America (series).
A. Richard Mansir (Charlesbridge Publishing)

The Story of Model T Fords. Classic Cars: An Imagination Library
Series (series). David Wright (Gareth Stevens Publishing)

Web Site

How Things Fly
www.nasm.si.edu/exhibitions/gal109/gal109.html
Learn how airplanes, balloons, and spacecraft fly at this site
of the Smithsonian National Air and Space Museum

Publisher's note to educators and parents: Our editors have carefully reviewed this
Web site to ensure that it is suitable for children. Many Web sites change frequently,
however, and we cannot guarantee that a site's future contents will continue to meet
our high standards of quality and educational value. Be advised that children should
be closely supervised whenever they access the Internet.

Index

About the Author

Dana Meachen Rau is the author of more than one hundred and fifty children's books, including nonfiction and books for early readers. She writes about history, science, geography, people, and even toys! She lives with her family in Burlington, Connecticut.